Top Surgery: Unbound

Top Surgery: Unbound

An Insider's Guide to Chest Masculinization Surgery

Drake Cameron Sterling, MSW

Sterling OmniMedia
Sausalito, California

Sterling OmniMedia, LLC
3020 Bridgeway, #357
Sausalito, CA 94965
www.topsurgeryunbound.com

Top Surgery: Unbound - An Insider's Guide to Chest Masculinization Surgery/Drake Cameron Sterling. -- 1st ed.

ISBN 13: 978-0-692660-27-0

To my wife, my co-conspirator in life's journey, and to my breasts, wherever they may be

I followed the trail out of the room, invigorated by the possibility of reinventing my own body. The meaning was mine, as long as I was with those who had the vision and vocabulary to understand my creation.
—Nick Krieger

Contents

Preface

O n my dresser I have a vintage Handy Andy Tool Set. It's a rectangular metal box with a picture of two young boys—one with a hammer and nail in his hands and a pencil behind his ear and the other in a baseball cap measuring something on a wooden bench. There are tools on the floor around them. The toolbox is red. And it's rusty, but I don't care. It's totally cool, and they are creating something, maybe even themselves.

This red metal toolbox is what inspired *Top Surgery: Unbound.* The tools I want to share with you come both from my personal experience with top surgery—in my case a double mastectomy with chest reconstruction—and from my background working in a hospital. As a medical social worker, I spent the better part of eight hours a day in a hospital, working in the intensive care unit and with surgery patients and those hospitalized for all kinds of reasons that aren't fun to think about.

Over the years, I've worked with hundreds of patients and their families, and with more doctors and nurses than I can count. My mornings started with rounds, where a team made up of professionals from various medical disciplines discussed each patient, head to toe, organ by organ. Every bodily fluid was accounted for and, yes, that was as disgusting as it sounds, especially in the morning. We had one rule: "no food analogies." You can imagine how that might ruin one's lunch.

I've seen wounds and complications from surgeries. I've seen patients who've made mistakes, for example not finishing a course of antibiotics, and ended up with a worsened condition—and I've seen doctors and nurses make mistakes, too. Doctors can be so focused on an illness and its cure that they cannot see the forest through the trees. I sometimes felt like the lone crusader championing the patient and the doctors' understanding of the person as a whole—sometimes gently, sometimes ferociously. I often educated patients about how to interact with hospital staff and ask questions about their condition, and encouraged them to be "compliant" with the treatment plan.

In many healthcare settings, LGBTQ patients have not been treated with respect or cultural competence. Fear of discrimination leads many of us to avoid caring for ourselves. Even staff who consider themselves open-minded often commit micro-aggressions that they are not aware of. I was fortunate to have the opportunity to provide diversity training to hospital staff, related to LGBTQ patients' needs. Providing a space for staff to safely ask questions and explore concepts such as gender was challenging, but also extremely gratifying, and I hope those talks contributed to the greater good.

Within the genderqueer community, we all know that language often fails us. How we refer to others has both cultural and time-sensitive elements. I've tried to use gender-neutral language with queer being my preferred umbrella term. Top surgery is not just for those transitioning from female to male but may include many other spectrums of gender, whether that is gender nonconforming, gender fluid, bi-gender, butch, and so on.

Admittedly, the writing is biased toward experiences in the United States, however most of the tools will still be relevant even if you are outside of the U.S.

I want to remind you that I am not a doctor. Every body is unique. For example, you may have preexisting conditions that change some of your options. Listen to your surgeon, ask questions, and get answers. It's a very intimate discussion and I believe this book will help you navigate the conversation with your physician and improve your experience.

My goal with *Top Surgery: Unbound* is to give you tools you can use to ask better questions, make good decisions, decrease any anxiety you might have, and help you prepare, before, during, and after your top surgery, so you can get the results you want.

If you've avoided the health care system, as many queer folks have (with valid reasons), you're going to have to jump in and be proactive. They have something you want; this is your body, and you need to express yourself clearly and understand what the medical system can and cannot do for you.

This book is full of tools—tools from an insider's perspective, suggestions you won't find on the Internet—to help you get that chest you've been longing for. This may be a new beginning for you, or it may be all you need to feel congruent. May the tools in this book help you remove the things that bind you, physically, emotionally, mentally, and spiritually, and empower you to create yourself—as many times as you want.

Drake Cameron Sterling, MSW
Marin County, California
March 2016

Acknowledgments

On my dresser, next to my vintage red toolbox, I've displayed two books: *The Butch/Femme Photo Project* and *Genderqueer and Other Identities.* Next to the bed is a copy of Rae Spoon and Ivan E. Coyote's book *Gender Failure.* In my heart, I carry the resonance of these books and other early works that were so validating for me—Leslie Feinberg's *Stone Butch Blues* and Kate Bornstein's *Gender Outlaws: On Men, Women and the Rest of Us.* The people in these books and these authors, these photographers—they are my heroes. They showed me, then and now, that I am not alone. They inspire me and help me to delve into, explore, and express my unique self, where it is and as it becomes. I am thankful that they took on their projects and shared them with the world.

I am also thankful to the folks that put up their

YouTube videos about top surgery and posted on their blogs about their surgery, and all those who uploaded pictures to TransBucket and other sites. These stories and pictures yelled, "Hey, you have possibilities, look what I did!" I learned something from so many of you and I find your courage admirable on the deepest level.

My wife has not only my heart but my deep gratitude, for allowing me time to write and encouraging me to take on new aspects of myself. She supported my surgery from the beginning and was there to help with bandages and pain medications. I hope you find someone to go through this journey with you, whether it's your partner, your mom, a friend, or even an online buddy.

Thank you to my son, Scott, and my daughter-in-law, Ylva, for their enthusiastic support and great ideas.

My spiritual teacher and healer of many years, Micheline Bogey, gets a big shout-out for helping me find peace, strength, clarity, and connection when I have most needed it.

Special thanks to the diverse staff at the Multispecialty Transitions Clinic in Oakland, California. Both in person and on the phone, they were warm and welcoming and answered so many of my questions. Dr. Chang's transparency about the process was educational and comforting. Dr. Karen Yokoo, my skilled surgeon, her amazing physician's assistant Thomas Greenwood, and the whole team are top-notch.

Thanks to Berta Bejarano for her leadership of a Diversity Committee I was proud to be part of. She and everyone there created such a welcoming and safe environment, encouraging us to be ourselves and to not accept being treated in anyway less-than.

Thanks to my editor, Teja Watson at Two Birds Editing, for her skillful guidance.

I am happy to have reconnected with an old friend, Lee, who so eloquently spoke about his personal journey of change in the last chapter and thank him for allowing us to peek into his experience with top surgery in such an intimate way.

I also want to thank my friends who called, asked questions, admitted to staring at my chest before and after surgery, stopped by and brought food during my recovery, and provided so much cheer and acceptance. It meant the world to me and I am convinced you helped me to recover faster.

Introduction

*E*veryone needs tools. Especially when it comes to a decision as personal and profound as having top surgery. As a medical social worker, I've worked in the health care system for well over a dozen years, with hundreds of patients, and beside a multitude of doctors. And yes, I've had top surgery myself.

I'll weave in parts of my story as a way to deliver information, but this book isn't about me. It's about providing you with insider information so you will be more informed and more likely to get the results you want from your surgery. I'll prepare you for the types of questions the therapist might ask you during that anxiety-provoking mental health assessment, and instruct you on how to interview surgeons, so you get the best person for the job. There are tools to help you prepare before, the day of, and after your surgery. I'll let you know how to best prepare yourself and your environment for optimum recovery. I'm going to let you know some of the reactions I got from colleagues, pre- and post-surgery, so that, if you are employed, the things people say do not catch you out. You may encounter people who need Diversity Training 101 at every step of this journey—I certainly did. Maybe it will be a teaching moment, or maybe you'll choose to just roll your eyes and stay focused on your mission.

The medical field is full of hierarchies, and the authority presented by people within that system can be intimidating. I would often encourage my patients to ask the doctor all of their questions and they would say, "I've never been through this, I don't even know what to ask." You don't know what you don't know, so I'll offer you some prompts. You might assume the doctor will tell you everything about what you are going to experience, but they won't. There will be surprises, and I'll write about those too.

This book does not assume that having top surgery means that you are transitioning to male. Lots of people get top surgery for lots of reasons and their gender identities are all over the map.

There are times when you might feel intimidated, anxious, or vulnerable. It is a surgery, after all, and you're going to under anesthesia, and you're going to be trusting a person who is virtually a stranger. And there will be pain. But even knowing all of that, I bet you are excited as hell. Just thinking about it puts a smile on your face. All of that is worth it, if you can have the body you've dreamt about for so long.

If there is one take-home message from this book, it is to be proactive about your surgery (and your health care in general). It is my hope that these tools will empower you as you move through this amazing transitional journey and experience the freedom of being unbound.

Chapter 1

These Breasts Are Not Mine

*E*ach morning as the shower blasted hot jets of water on my back, I placed my hands on my breasts and pressed them flat. And I would always ask myself the same question: "Where did these come from? When did this happen?" They felt so foreign to me, still, after all these years.

I love clothes, specifically men's clothes, but getting dressed took some work. Having tried many forms of binding over the years, I finally ended up using a compression sports bra, always a little too tight, usually followed by a T-shirt and then a men's button-down shirt, which was always one size bigger to accommodate the breasts that seemed to be growing bigger as I got older.

Top surgery is a gender-affirming surgery that removes breast tissue and sculpts the remaining tissue into what is typically considered a more male-appearing chest. I had thought about having top surgery for years. I talked about it a lot, and I talked about my reasons for not doing it. Working in an intensive care unit, I tend to see the surgeries that are more complicated, or maybe didn't go so well, or people who aren't healing properly for a myriad of reasons. My conclusion was "do not do elective surgery." I reasoned that I didn't HAVE to have top surgery; it wasn't worth the risk. (Never mind that I didn't have a backlog of medical problems and was pretty healthy.)

Next on my "List of Reasons I Am Not Going to Have This Surgery" was my age. It wasn't like I was in my twenties anymore, and I lamented that the time for surgery had passed. Maybe if I were younger. Which of course is a myth as people get top surgery at many different ages.

I also wondered if I would have to give up my butch identity, which I felt so grounded in. It connected me to those who came before me and held me steady in the present. I remember one of my friends saying I was a unicorn—"It's very hard to find a butch because they're all transitioning," she said. Would this make me some kind of traitor?

I also cross-examined myself to see if removing my breasts was some sort of internalized misogyny. Still, the fantasies of imagining how I would look without breasts persisted. With more frequency I went on the Internet and researched surgeons and studied pictures. The time for change was getting closer, though I didn't know it yet.

A "Lesbians Who Tech" conference was an unlikely setting for me to change course. My wife had wanted me to join her at the conference, but I had mixed feelings about going. I'm not a techie, but the conference was open to women in tech and those who love them. I wanted to be supportive.

So there we were, watching this diverse group of women, all with laptops, iPads, and iPhones in hand, listening to speaker after speaker. It was actually more interesting than I had anticipated.

Then a group of life coaches came onto the stage. They took turns giving their spiels and one said she helped people with life transitions, including gender transitions. I wasn't expecting that, and suddenly my interest was piqued. Just hearing those words—*gender transitions*—created a stirring inside me.

On the break we went for a walk around our San Francisco venue, with the bay reflecting sunlight on our right and a variety of tall and short buildings on our left. We played that game—you know, the one that goes, "If I won the lottery today I would…"—and out of my mouth popped "I would go see that surgeon in Florida and have top surgery." Hearing my own words, I then said, "Wait, I have health insurance that will pay for this. I *have* won the lottery. I'm going to do it."

Helen was in agreement. The decision was made right then and there, and I didn't look back. Any fears I had were replaced by excitement and anticipation.

That decision set off a domino effect of dealing with the insurance company, a mental health assessment, meeting and interviewing surgeons, my partner's reaction, preparing for surgery, deciding whom to tell, and building my support team. Then, finally, handling the day of surgery and getting through the postoperative period.

There were many things that happened that took me by surprise, but don't worry, when you finish this book, you will be in much better shape than I was—you'll be more informed, feel less vulnerable, and be empowered to make decisions regarding your body.

A note about insurance: regardless of whether you have insurance or are paying privately, the information in this book will be helpful. If you are working, and qualify to apply for some time off through disability, I encourage you to apply as early as possible. It can be a complicated process. If you can afford it, don't be in such a hurry to get back to work—it is a big surgery and giving yourself time to heal is okay!

I am privileged enough to have insurance that pays for top surgery (more and more of them do), but I still had to jump through a few hoops. When looking into whether or not your insurance will cover the cost, call a few times, talk to different people in different departments such as membership services, your primary care physician, OB/GYN department, mental health and plastic surgery., Try using the words "I am seeking treatment for gender dysphoria" or "gender identity disorder." Don't just say, "I want to know if you will cover a double mastectomy."

There are still many reasons people seeking top surgery need financial assistance, including being a student, loss of employment, or being on a limited income. If you cannot get the cost of your surgery covered by insurance, then consider asking the doctor for a payment plan, or try community fund-raising. Occasionally retailers offer contests to assist with funds for top surgery. Some have family that will chip in and offer financial support. When I went to college I signed up for some medical studies and made some decent money in the name of science. Sell stuff on eBay, move to a cheaper apartment, do whatever it takes, but do not give up—you will find a way!

With my insurance, everything starts with a referral from one's primary care physician (PCP). Bless his heart, he had absolutely no idea what I was talking about. It was both frustrating and comical, and worth sharing to prepare you for such encounters.

My PCP referred me to Plastics (a.k.a. the plastic surgery department). I called them and told the person answering the phone what I was interested in, in the simplest way I could: "a double mastectomy related to gender transition." I was put on hold.

Now, mind you, I was new at verbalizing this, so I was nervous and pacing. The person returned to the line and said, "So this is your second mastectomy?" Where on earth did she come up with that? No.

Then she said, "So you don't have cancer?" No. "Well, we cannot remove all of the breast tissue, we have to leave 10 percent, so we can't help you and I'm not sure where to refer you." End of conversation.

What? Seriously? My PCP and this person in Plastics were the first people I had approached, and I was already being cock-blocked. This is when we practice our deep breathing. Breathe in, hold to count of five, release. It will do you well to remember this exercise, as you'll likely have to do it again and again.

If you experience these kind of people, who are not educated, I know you, dear reader, will not get derailed—you will keep calling, keep knocking, keep asking, keep researching, because having made the decision to get top surgery and you will not be thwarted by someone else.

Months earlier, I had heard about a gender transitions clinic within my HMO, when a friend encouraged me to apply for a job there, but I had not reached out to them. My wife was able to track down the number online. I called them and they directed me to have my PCP refer me directly to them, which I did. He thanked me for being patient with him and made the referral to the specialty clinic.

Remember, there are a lot of moving parts in the medical system, so you'll need to be persistent and ready to handle some uninformed people along the way. If you're going to a private surgeon who specializes in top surgery, one benefit is that the process will be more streamlined and the people you deal with will be more informed.

While I was waiting for my appointment, I wanted to make SURE my policy would cover the surgery, so I called Member Services. I had to tell them what I wanted done, so again I referred to a "double mastectomy due to gender transition," hoping that would explain it. The response was a surprised "What?" Pause. "Oh!" Pause. "Well…" Pause. "I guess you've thought this through." And yes, my policy covered the surgery. Then: "Good luck." I knew I had more than good luck—I had insurance coverage!

Chapter 2

The Mental Health Assessment Demystified

*H*istorically, queer people have collectively been stigmatized by the medical and mental health field—so when we're about to enter both of them, it's disconcerting at best. In this chapter we'll focus on the metal health assessment.

More than likely, you will need one letter from a mental health professional, with their recommendation stating that you are stable for top surgery. That requirement alone will make some people see red. It seems absurd that we need a gatekeeper to give us permission to do something to our bodies that makes us feel good about ourselves. It's righteous anger. Give yourself a minute to be pissed off, then move on, because you want the surgery and someone else wrote the rule book.

Let's unravel this a bit. Many doctors follow the World Professional Association for Transgender Health (WPATH) guidelines, which defines a Standard of Care (SOC) or "best practice." Following a standard of care means that the physician could argue in court that they acted in accordance with what a reasonably prudent person would do under similar circumstances. The recommendation of WPATH as a SOC in this context is for a mental health screening or assessment—not psychotherapy, just an assessment. It also protects the patient from some doctor going rogue, as they could be held accountable for not following a SOC.

For most of us, the idea of seeing a therapist makes us feel anxious. This practitioner is the gatekeeper for your surgery, so no wonder it feels scary. My own mind was barraged with questions: Would I be turned away? Was my fate in this one therapist's hands? Would it be some random therapist connected with my insurance company who was clueless about gender issues? What kinds of questions would they ask me? How should I answer to optimize my chances for surgery?

If your mind is spinning, let me try to put it at ease. It helps to understand the role of the therapist. Basically, what they are trying to do is assess your mental readiness for such a transition. It's not intended to be a barrier. At worst, they might say "not now, let's do a couple of sessions and create a plan." It's not likely they will outright say "no." So, if you are depressed or bipolar, the therapist might want to ensure that you are stable on your medications. If you are not living in one place but couch surfing, they may want to ensure that you have a safe postoperative plan. Maybe your partner or your parents are against the surgery; the therapist might then help you work through that situation. Overall, the therapist should be helping you identify your strengths and resources. They should be on your side.

Here is WPATH's "criteria for mastectomy and creation of a male chest in FtM patients":

1. Persistent, well-documented gender dysphoria;
2. Capacity to make a fully informed decision and to consent for treatment;
3. Age of majority in a given country (if younger, follow the SOC for children and adolescents);
4. If significant medical or mental health concerns are present, they must be reasonably well controlled.

This gives you an idea of what the clinician will be documenting in their letter and how their questions will help them frame your gender dysphoria.

I'd like to make an important point here and that is to remember that you may have a choice about who will perform this assessment. Perhaps you already have a therapist who can provide this letter to your surgeon—perfect! Perhaps your point of entry is your primary care doctor, who will advise you to call the mental health department; perhaps you are working with a local, private surgeon who specializes in top surgery, and they will give you a list of mental health providers in the area—or if they are in another state than you are, they may send you to your physician for a referral. My point is that you do not have to accept the first person on the list. Get several names, their location, their gender, and even their percentage of evaluations that went through without further appointments if you can. You can then see if they have an online presence and see whether they might be a good match for you.

I had a prescreening phone interview to set up my mental health appointment, at which time they asked me how I identified and the pronoun I preferred. They sent me a questionnaire to fill out, with past medical history and current medications—very generic.

There was one burning question I had, and I used this phone call as a chance to ask, so I would be ready with the "right answer" for the in-person meeting. I wanted to know if I should say that I wanted to be male. This is obviously an important question for anyone who is gendervariant, genderqueer, gender nonconforming, or who is not sure.

Thankfully, the answer to this is that non-binary people, those who are outside the gender binary of male and female, can get top surgery. WPATH's version 7 SOC does state that it's okay to not be on the gender binary, but I didn't know that at the time. The person on the phone eased my mind, saying the top surgery evaluation is pretty straightforward; it gets more complex with bottom surgery.

It is also good to know that hormone therapy is not a prerequisite. If you are under age 18 in the United States, you will need parental/guardian consent.

When you set up your appointment, it is a good time to ask if you will be told the therapist's recommendation at the end of the session or if you will have to wait for a call back. Having that information will greatly reduce your anxiety.

At the end of my session, the therapist told me that if I agreed, I would now have a diagnosis of gender dysphoria, and she would recommend me for surgery. I accepted the diagnosis, because it moves this surgery out of the realm of elective surgery to a necessary treatment, which means my insurance, and maybe yours, will pay.

Gender dysphoria refers to distress caused by the difference between how you see your gender identity versus your assigned sex at birth. I had plenty of distress around this over the years—that I could not deny. Was I happy about getting labeled by the mental health profession? Certainly not. Was I willing to take the label to get the surgery paid for? Yes.

However, all of that said, if you are absolutely against this step, it is possible to find surgeons who provide top surgery without a letter from a mental health provider, though they will likely be private-pay surgeons and more difficult to track down. You will want to look for someone who operates under "informed consent" guidelines. In short, informed consent means that you understand the procedure and the risks and benefits.

After my session, I took my label and left the office. The rapid-fire ping pong of questions and answers each collided with pockets of memories filled with hurt, confusion, anger, and pain, leaving me feeling raw and vulnerable. What took me a lifetime to work through was compressed into an hour-long life review, and my head and body were spinning, not unlike the after-effects of gulping a strong cocktail. *Do I feel euphoric or am I going to throw up?*

As I walked down the street, barely dodging oncoming baby strollers and hands darting out asking for money, the screech of car brakes brought me into my body. I shook off the old memories like a dog after a bath and allowed myself to feel the exhilaration of it all.

I couldn't drive right away; I knew that much. I went for a walk, took deep breaths, and called my wife. Remember this, readers: take some time to ground yourself afterward. It's an intense inquiry and may stir up some deep emotions.

To help you prepare for the mental health assessment, I've created a list of topics that are likely to be covered in your session.

Twenty-One Questions the Therapist Might Ask You

1. How do you identify in terms of gender?
2. What surgery are you interested in, and what makes this seem like the right time to have it?
3. Tell me when you first noticed your gender.
4. How was school for you?
5. What was it like growing up?
6. What did your parents think about your gender presentation?
7. What was your relationship with your father as it related to gender?
8. What was your relationship with your mother as it related to gender?
9. Who do you consider your family to be?
10. If you have a partner, how do they feel about you having top surgery?
11. Will you tell your parent(s), sibling(s)?
12. Who will provide support after the surgery?
13. Do you know anyone who has had top surgery or identifies as trans?

14. How much alcohol do you drink on an average week?
15. Do you use any recreational drugs or smoke cigarettes?
16. Do you want to go on hormone therapy?
17. Do you plan to have bottom surgery?
18. If you are employed, how long do you plan to be off work?
19. What medications are you currently taking?
20. Have you had any other surgery? If so, what was it like?
21. What do you expect from having chest reconstruction surgery? How do you think it will change your life?

Even though I had combed the Internet before my surgery, I didn't find anything that prepared me for this assessment. I'm not saying it's going to be painless, and I'm not presenting the questions here to help you work the system. Rather, my intention is to ease your mind by taking away some of the mystery.

Chapter 3

Improve Your Chances of Hiring the Best Surgeon

*T*his is a big surgery, and you don't want to end up on an episode of *Botched,* right? Finding a surgeon is not the type of decision you want to make based only on a doctor's website or a few pictures they've posted on the Internet.

I do think there's value in reading reviews from people who have used a particular surgeon and checking out pictures their patients have posted. In fact, I think the people who have done that are incredibly generous, and it certainly helped me during my exploration phase—both as a visual of what I would or wouldn't want and as a way to manage my expectations.

And please don't make your decision solely based on price. There are many factors to consider when choosing a surgeon.

If you're using insurance, you will likely be given the names of surgeons who are available to do this procedure. If you're paying privately, you can look on the Internet for names and reviews. But remember, all that glitters is not gold. Some doctors with slick websites might be poor surgeons, and many competent surgeons don't have good marketing or Internet chops.

A great approach is to get a referral from a friend whose top surgery results you like. You might also check in with some trans support groups or agencies who work with trans clients, or an LGBT center if your community has one. If you can go to a trans conference, they sometimes have surgery workshops or speakers, and this can be a great way to make connections. Whether you want a surgeon who is local, or have the ability to travel, may also impact your decision.

The first thing to do, once you have a few names, is to check the American Board of Plastic Surgery's site to make sure they are board-certified (abplasticsurgery.org) in plastic surgery, which has its own standards and training. That site will also link to your state's medical board, so you can see if the doctor has had any disciplinary actions against them. Just for fun, I randomly picked a guy in

Florida who advertised low-priced top surgery (a red flag in and of itself). When I went to the Florida Board of Medicine, it turned out he had disciplinary actions against him, which I could read in detail. This is good information to have.

I recommend you interview two or three surgeons, but definitely more than one. Meeting with them in person is best, if at all possible. If you're interviewing a surgeon who is out of state over the phone—or better yet, on Skype—think about also interviewing someone local who offers a free consultation. This will give you perspective and help you to go back and ask better questions of the out-of-state doctor.

In my case, I narrowed my selection down to two surgeons, and even though they worked for the exact same HMO, I was totally surprised when they each had completely different techniques and opposite personalities.

Questions to Ask Yourself before You Meet with the Surgeon

When would I prefer to have the surgery?

Take a look at your calendar and think about taking several weeks off work (usually two to four, depending on the type of work you do). Here's an insider tip from someone who worked in a hospital: Do not schedule your surgery on a Friday or holiday weekend, as the doctor and staff may not be available should you have a complication. Don't do it during a big sports event weekend like the Super Bowl or the World Series—lots of staff call off on those weekends. The score of the game, not you, will be their focus. And schedule your appointment first thing in the morning, when the surgeon will be fresh and not running late from other surgeries.

Also consider how long you want to wait. Some of the best surgeons have a year to a year-and-a-half wait list. And of course, avoid Shark Week if you can—that is, if you still have a period. If you can avoid scheduling surgery during that week, your life will obviously be easier. You won't be able to swim, get in a jacuzzi or expose your chest to direct sunlight for many months so you might want to delay those beach vacation plans.

What is more important to me—bedside manner and feeling comfortable with the person, or skill set and competency?

I know that doesn't seem fair. I hope you won't have to decide between the two. Hopefully you can get both in the same person, but just have the answer to this question in the back of your mind in case you have to lean one way or the other. It is crucial that you ask your potential doctors how many top surgeries they have performed. In my case, one of the surgeons was so sweet, kind, and caring. She assured me she would be there for me anytime, even long after the surgery. I bonded with her immediately. But when I asked her how many surgeries like this she had done, she answered "less than five." The other surgeon I interviewed had a brusque personality; she grabbed my breasts and pulled and pushed and pinched. I could see the wheels turning in her mind as she contemplated what would need to be done to create my new chest. She had an air of confidence and was intimidating, though I'm sure that wasn't intentional. The two doctors also had very different techniques, which I'll get to in a minute, but it made the decision difficult.

I ran it by many of my hospital co-workers, and in the end we all agreed that skill set is more important than personality or bedside manner. However, that said, you need to feel respected and heard by the surgeon, whether or not they seem arrogant. They need to care about you and the look you want.

How important is the gender of the doctor?

This can be complicated by past traumas such as rape or incest. You're already going to be vulnerable—why add another layer of difficulty?

Readers: be prepared to be fondled. This is a land mine for many of us. Maybe you're not used to having your breasts touched; maybe you don't even refer to them as breasts (but the doctor will). At the very least, you will likely feel exposed and vulnerable. I want you to be ready. Take a deep breath and stay as grounded as you can, so you can

33

listen and ask your questions (they're on the list in your back pocket).

I had two very different experiences with the surgeons I interviewed. One opened my gown, took a polite look, barely touched one breast, then closed the gown and said that, yes, she could do the surgery, it wouldn't be a problem. The other surgeon—I thought maybe she was trying to pick a ripe fruit for dessert. She did a lot of pinching at the chest wall, she compared left to right sides.

Consider whether you want to be alone in the exam room, to have privacy, or whether you might want someone with you for support, or so you have a second set of ears taking in information. If you can tolerate it, I suggest having someone there with you during the exam; they can stay present, take notes, and ask the questions you forgot to ask.

Practically speaking, it's good to have a notebook to write down the things the doctor says. Believe me, there will be a lot of information and it will be hard to remember exactly what was said. You can also use this to write down your medications post-surgery, to keep track of which ones you've taken and when. Get a folder to put all the paperwork in, as there will be release forms and insurance forms and discharge instructions, etc. It will be easier to keep them all in one place.

Doctors are generally not chatter-bugs; they are a focused bunch, especially surgeons. While I encourage you to ask lots of questions, be direct with your questions and short with your answers when they ask you something. This is not the time for long, personal storytelling.

When you meet with the surgeon, take a look around and make sure the place is clean. Look around the office, use the bathroom, check that they are washing their hands or using sanitizing gel before touching you. Of course the operating room will be sterile, but how they act here is a good indication of their standards of practice.

Questions to Ask Your Prospective Surgeons

1. Do they use drains?

What, you didn't know there was a choice? I didn't either! One of the surgeons I interviewed used drains and one did not. In fact, when I asked the second surgeon I interviewed about drains she said, "I've evolved my practice; my patients have done fine without them." Damn. Okay.

So what is a drain? In top surgery, a drain is used to prevent the accumulation of fluid from your surgical site. They usually stay in for five to seven days. It's a little uncomfortable coming out, and the longer they stay in the more uncomfortable that will be. They are usually removed when the fluid collection has slowed down or stopped. If yours is really irritating, it can be removed early, so be sure to call your surgeon if that's the case.

Surgeons have been using drains for a long

time, but their efficacy is not without controversy. On one hand, you'll be told they help reduce infection and promote healthy wound healing. On the other hand, you may be told that the evidence of this is inconsistent and that drains can actually provide a pathway for infection, especially as the days go by, and if you are not careful to use clean techniques.

I saw a lot of drains, working in the hospital, and it was common to hear the infectious disease doctor press, "Can the drains come out yet?" To them, removing them meant one less path for infection.

Most surgeons still use drains for top surgery, but it helps to know that you might have the option of no drains, especially as top surgery evolves. Discuss this with your surgeon. It makes home care much easier, especially if you or your caregiver get queasy in dealing with bodily fluids.

2. How do they plan to help you with pain control post-operation?

This was another big difference between the surgeons I met with. Surgeon number one was going to insert a pain pump for a few days, then I would go back to her to have it removed. A pain pump in this situation would've been either an IV or a pump placed under my skin which delivers medication either continuously or when I push the button. This does not seem to be a common practice for top surgery.

Surgeon number two told me that she chose to cut ever so slightly above the pectoral muscle and that this has meant less pain and quicker healing for her patients. Common pain medications prescribed are hydrocodone (Norco, Vicodin) and oxycodone (OxyContin, Percocet).

3. Will you have a choice about the shape of the scar?

For example, I knew I was having a double incision, but the doctor left it to me to decide if I wanted a straight line cut or a curved one, and how much curve. This is also a good time to ask about their recommendations for scar treatment.

I was also crystal clear that I did not want a flat or concave chest, and I repeated this a couple of times to ensure we were on the same page. I wanted her to contour a male chest with pecs.

4. Do they have any before and after surgery pictures that you can look at?

This is especially helpful if they have pictures of someone close to your before-surgery size so you can see the results this surgeon had.

While we're on the subject, as far as having pictures taken of you before and after surgery, there are several consent forms you will have to sign, and one of the questions will be permission to take pictures. It may be sandwiched in between a lot of other things, so be sure to not give consent if you do not want them to take pictures. This can be done by simply crossing out that paragraph and initialing it.

5. What about your nipples?

At some point during the interview the surgeon will have a recommendation for the type of surgery they believe would be best for you and this includes the nipple treatment.

Of course you will have lots of questions about your nipples: Will they retain any sensation? What technique do they use on the nipples? What are the options? What can you expect them to look like? How will they determine size and placement?

6. What can you expect as far as scheduling your surgery?

Some doctors have a long wait list; others can get you in sooner. If that's an important consideration for you, you may want to even ask on your initial phone consultation. You can also ask about when they conduct post-op visits and how many you can expect; you may need to arrange transportation. Don't forget to ask when they think you can return to work, if applicable. Doctors often minimize recovery time, so please be sure to give yourself as much time to heal as you possibly can.

Ask if revisions are included in the cost. Sometimes, especially with private pay surgeons, a revision is covered but not the cost of the anesthesiologist or the surgical facilities.

Ultimately, you have to trust the surgeon

you select. Once you're under anesthesia, you have no voice. So ask your questions and express yourself before the procedure. There are no stupid questions. Don't be intimidated. This is your body. You want to feel like they hear you and they're going to do what you want, to the best of their ability. The scalpel is in their hand, but the choice is yours.

Chapter 4

Control Your Results by Knowing Your Surgical Options

*T*he operation you're about to undergo is technically called a "subcutaneous mastectomy." "Subcutaneous" means "under the skin," and "mastectomy" refers to the surgical removal of breast tissue. The plastic surgeon will also be contouring a male chest, and that is the real magic.

The decision about which type of surgery you will have depends mostly on the size of your breasts and your skin elasticity—your skin's ability to bounce back to its original shape when pulled. Poor elasticity can come from age, excess sun exposure, smoking, genetics, and diet. Binding, over a long period of time, can also have an influence on skin elasticity.

The surgeon will also consider the overall state of your health, whether you've had other surgeries before—and if so, how you did with healing and scarring—as well as your body weight and how it might influence the overall result.

The discussion about surgery type is important, so that your expectations are in alignment with what the doctor can provide. There was a picture of a guy with a cool haircut in a magazine. I ripped the page out and took it into my stylist and said, "I want to look like this." She laughed and said, "Well, I can cut your hair like that but you won't look like him!" Likewise, you and your surgeon need to be on the same page about what is possible.

We'll cover several of the most common surgical procedures here, so you can have a sense of the options available to you, and prepare for your surgical consultation. As I've mentioned, the recommended surgical procedure is generally based on breast size and skin elasticity, but it also includes how to handle the "NAC," a term doctors use to refer to your "nipple areola complex." The actual nipple is the protruding tip (unless yours are inverted), and the areola is the darker-colored skin around it. Of course, everyone's NAC varies in size. What is done with your NAC will have an impact on whether you retain sensation—most, some, or minimal.

Keyhole

Those of you with small breasts and good skin elasticity may qualify for the Keyhole technique. With this method, a small incision is made along the bottom of the areola and the breast tissue is removed via liposuction. Drains, if used, are inserted through the incision and slid under the pectoral area, coming out via two small incisions at each of your armpits. So that's four total cuts plus lipo.

The good news with this technique is that it leaves a very small scar and your nipples will likely maintain much of their sensation. Liposuction is the wild card here, and might have an effect on some of the nerves, resulting in some sensation loss.

The NAC is usually not initially resized in this method and the skin is not tightened. If the aesthetic you end up with is not exactly what you were hoping for, you could opt for a surgical revision after six to eight months.

Periareolar Incision

Periareolar Incision is often lumped together with Keyhole on the Internet, but they are two different kinds of surgeries. Periareolar, around the areola, Incision might be recommended for you if you have a B- or C-cup size and good chest skin elasticity. With this method, an incision is made around the entire circumference of the areola. Breast tissue is then removed, leaving as much of the nerve tissue and blood supply (sometimes called "nipple stalk," or "pedicle") attached to the body—with the goal being for you to retain some sensation.

The areola may be trimmed to reduce its size. Excess skin on the chest may also be removed, along the circumference of the incision. The skin is then pulled tight toward the center of the opening and the nipple is reattached to the areola — similar to closing a drawstring, which explains why this procedure is sometimes referred to as the "drawstring" or "purse string" technique and may result in some puckering around the incision. The NAC may also be repositioned slightly, depending on original breast size and the available skin. This procedure will result in a scar around the circumference of the areola. As with the keyhole procedure, the drains will exit via the armpits.

Double Incision

So you've got some big bad double DD's dragging you down? Then Double Incision (DI) is the surgery for you and any of your friends who happen to be a C to D+ and/or have poor skin elasticity.

To be honest, I had no idea what my cup size was; the thought of cup size didn't feel like it applied to me, since I couldn't remember the last time a bought a bra with actual cups. All I knew was that I needed an XL-size sports bra.

DI is a dramatic surgery in which long horizontal incisions (I have two nine-inch scars) are made on the lower part of your chest. You may be able to choose the shape of the incision (curved or straight), and thus the shape of the scar, so be sure to ask your surgeon.

Tissue is removed and contouring done (think scalpel and liposuction). If your doctor is using drains, the thin tubing will be put in along the incision line and will exit near the armpits. Skin will be trimmed to fit your new chest and dissolving stitches will be used to put you back together. Those will be covered with steri-strips, which will stay on until they fall off on their own or they may be removed at your follow-up appointment.

As far as your nipples go, the most common technique used with DI is the free nipple graft, in which the NAC is completely removed, trimmed, then grafted onto your new chest. Since your nipples are severed from the nerves, they will not retain their *original* sensation. I'm sorry. Your current and future lovers are sorry. Some people do report that, in time, they have regained some reaction to touch or cold. You may cry now. I have seen some YouTube videos by people who say that they have sensation after a DI. I hope this will be you.

There is another risk for your nipples. Not all grafts are successful, resulting in the NAC, or part of it, dying and falling off. There is not always a reason, it just sometimes happens. My understanding is that it can result from loss of blood flow, infection, swelling, or over-stretching and pulling on the stitches, or the stitches getting too dry. But listen, please find some comfort in the fact that most of the time these grafts are successful. If you feel like they are not healing properly, immediately reach out to your doctor so that they can do whatever is possible to save your graft. Early intervention is crucial.

I had one nipple-related complication, which was that one nipple bled through the bandages. We sent a photo to the surgeon, who said it was normal and not to worry. However, a couple days later the blood was still seeping, so we sent another pic, at which point she said to come on in and they

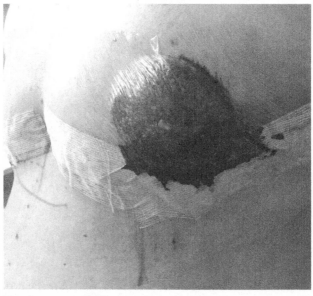

Bandage over NAC saturated with blood

would take a look. The nipple was re-bandaged and it was fine.

Tip: Always err on the side of caution. Do not feel like you are bothering them. This is your body and your peace of mind. If something does not feel or look right to you, please, please ask your doctor, several times if you have to.

If the grafts do not take, you can have nipples tattooed on, or there are people who choose to have no nipples. I don't say this lightly, it's disappointing and scary to have that happen but getting your body well is your first priority then you can explore options like tattoos.

Here's a tidbit you can take comfort in. I had DI and lost my nipple sensation as predicted, which was sad for both my wife and me. I did regain some sensation after time but it was not the same. However, to our surprise and happiness, my entire chest became an erogenous zone. Initially it was the tingling of nerves reconnecting, but later I think it was just me feeling more comfortable in my body—not just more comfortable but more congruent and more in and into my body. Whatever the reason, it was a nice surprise.

You may have heard or read about the term "dog ears." This can be a problem with the DI surgery. It refers to flaps of skin that hang down near the armpits. Not everyone gets them, but if you do, and they are bothering you, you may want a revision done to take care of them. Again, you'll have to wait six to eight months.

Inverted-T

The Inverted-T, also known as the T-Anchor, is effective for those with B or larger size breasts and poor skin elasticity. It starts out similar to the Double Incision method, with those two long horizontal cuts. In addition, there is a vertical incision made between the lower part of your areola and that horizontal cut, creating an upside down T. The idea is to keep the NAC attached to its original blood and nerve supply (pedicle), so as to preserve as much sensation as possible. The NAC can still be trimmed and repositioned somewhat, and your chances of keeping your NAC are improved, since it is not a nipple graft as it is in the DI procedure. While the incision is open, breast tissue will be removed, your new chest sculpted and drains, if used, will be placed.

Other Considerations

Are you thinking about having a breast reduction, because insurance will cover it, and then having top surgery at a later date? Please talk to a plastic surgeon before you do this, as a breast reduction may impact what your top surgery options are.

Do you think you might ever want to have and nurse a baby? Some people might be able to have top surgery and retain the ability to nurse if the posterior pedicle is preserved. I am not sure a surgeon would guarantee this but it is worth a conversation if a baby is in your future.

Surgery comes with probable outcomes, risks, and no guarantees. With the right tools you can mindfully go forward with the surgery option that's best for you.

Chapter 5

Tactical Moves to Prepare for Surgery

*I*n this chapter we're going to look at strategies for gathering support, setting up your home, packing your bag for your surgery day, preparing for travel if your surgery is out of town and even preparing for emergencies. With a little advanced planning you will be ready for your big day.

I was so excited about my decision to get top surgery that I told a few friends and coworkers. They were excited for me, but fumbled over their words. They had questions and I tried to answer them. "Will we still call you this name or will you have another?" "What pronoun should we use afterward?" Although at first I only told a few people, it was hard to contain my enthusiasm. After a while I couldn't remember who knew and who didn't. Then those people told people and pretty soon everyone was staring at my chest. Once the word is out, don't kid yourself into thinking it will stay underground.

My closest friends shared my excitement, but many of the people I told about my top surgery gasped and asked, "It's not cancer, is it?" When I said no and tried to explain the surgery, their expressions went from concerned to puzzled. They didn't exactly know what to say or how to react. Not that I blame them, they just didn't seem to have any experience with this kind of surgery or even with discussing anything related to gender. I live in this world but they don't so I was able to have some understanding and do some education.

"Will you tell your family?" This was a question the therapist asked me. I decided not to tell my mother and brother. I didn't feel great about this, but it felt too personal, too vulnerable. These are not things my family talks about. They live in another state, and when we talked on the phone, and they asked what I was up to, the topic of my surgery almost slipped out several times. I always caught myself and said "Oh, nothing." All those years I'd spent trying to develop an authentic relationship with them was down the tubes, and it was on me. I felt guilty.

One day, several months after the surgery, I had a T-shirt on and walked by a mirror and saw myself. I was pleased—finally a T-shirt looks good on me! Then it hit me. We were flying my mom out for Thanksgiving, and there was no way she could NOT notice that my globes were gone. I hoped I could count on our unspoken family rules about not discussing intimate matters. Over that holiday I was so self conscious. I rehearsed what I might say if she brought it up with my best line being, "Oh those old things, I didn't need them anymore." I will never know if she noticed or not, the topic hasn't come up to this day.

I did tell my adult son, and it was awkward. He didn't ask any questions, but just said, "That's great! Good luck." I'm not sure what I was expecting from the poor guy; I wanted him to know in advance of the surgery in case something went wrong.

I also told my two sisters-in-law at lunch, between bites of salad. No one choked. I felt like I was coming out all over again. I reasoned that it was smart to tell them because it would give my wife extra support, but really it was just that I was bubbling over with anticipation and excitement. They seemed happy for me, or maybe they were just being polite. One of them sent flowers after my surgery with a sweet card from the family (Had she told her husband and kids?). I was touched. It was thoughtful and kind.

My wife told a friend without asking me. One of my friends also told a mutual friend; she didn't ask me either. My reaction was stupid. "Hey, this is my body. I'm not ready for everyone to know. It's my body; don't I get to decide who gets to know and when?" I guess I was being a control freak. My surgery affected them too, especially my wife. They needed their own support.

You may have reasons not to tell your family, or you may want to shout it from the rooftops. Whatever you decide, there's no right or wrong. It's about your comfort and safety.

Of course, there is too much time to think between the time you decide you want to have surgery and the actual day of surgery. I wondered if my wife would accept my new chest, if she would be able to see beyond the scars. Would I be ready if, in the worst-case scenario, it came between us, and created distance? In the end, she was more amazing than I ever could've hoped for. Understanding, patient, and the best caregiver, writing down the medications, making me take them when I didn't want to, reminding me not to reach for things, driving me to appointments, and being emotionally available.

After the surgery, my friends texted, called, and stopped by. They dropped off food, they looked at the before and after pictures I proudly showed them in my doped-on-pain-pills state. I felt held in that space and celebrated. And very, very thankful.

Remember I said that the therapist would ask you what kind of support you have in your life? Before surgery, you should give this some thought.

Many of us have had to be tough to survive. We may be guarded. We will be the first to pull over and help change a tire or offer a ride to someone, but when the tables are turned it can be hard to be vulnerable and accept help. But here's the thing—when you help someone you feel pretty good, right? Let your supporters feel good, and accept their offers to help out. Don't try to be a tough guy and do this on your own. Maybe, like me, you're afraid you're not worthy, or they won't show up. Let them surprise you.

There are some other things you will need to gather before your surgery. You may need to get lab tests or have a mammogram. If you are using a private plastic surgeon or going out of state, the doctor may require a letter from your primary care physician giving you medical clearance to go forward with the procedure. If you are taking testosterone (T), the surgeon will likely recommend that you ask your PCP if they want you to continue taking it, or stop for a brief period of time.

You have probably heard the term HIPAA, which stands for Health Insurance Portability and Accountability Act. HIPAA is a set of regulations designed to protect your private health information, and will require you to sign a form giving consent to the doctor to speak with others and provide them with medical information. You can put a time limit on this form (three months should be sufficient) and you can limit the types of information they can discuss. For example, you can ask them to withhold information about mental health, alcohol and drug use, HIV status, and/or photos. This form will be provided by the doctor's office. You'll need to sign this form if you want to enable the doctor to speak with the person accompanying you to the surgery, or a friend or family member asking for information on your behalf.

If you smoke tobacco, be prepared for them to recommend that you quit. At minimum, there should be no smoking two weeks before and several weeks after your surgery. Smoking decreases blood flow and impedes the body's ability to deliver oxygen to all those tissues. This slows healing of wounds and increases the chance of infection. Remember, those nipple grafts are fragile and need all the help they can get. And hell, if you quit for six weeks you might as well just quit period.

Another thing to consider is how well you tolerate pain and what pain medications have or have not worked for you in the past. One of the questions you're likely to get from the doctor or nurse is, "On a scale of one to ten, what level of pain are you okay with?" Don't be a hero here—pain meds are going to be your best friend for the first few days after your surgery.

Regarding other medications and vitamins you may take regularly, the doctor or their staff will go over those with you beforehand. They may want you to quit taking certain things such as ibuprofen and fish oil, which tend to thin the blood. You'll also want to mention any latex or other allergies you have.

If you have nipple piercings, plan ahead and get non-metal retainers or spacers. You will need to remove all of your piercings and jewelry before surgery. There are multiple reasons for that, including accidental harm, such as a sheet or gown catching on a piercing and ripping your skin. There is also the potential for burns, since metal conducts heat and they are likely using an instrument that uses heat (called "electrocautery") during the surgery. If there is an emergency and you have to be taken for an MRI, the last thing the medical team needs to worry about is getting metal out of your body so you can go into a scanner. There is swelling after surgery, as well as the potential for lost jewelry while you're either under or loopy on medication. I had to take off my wedding ring for the surgery and gave it to my wife, who wore it on her necklace for safe keeping during my procedure. When we got home she gave it to me, but I was high on pain medication. I think I put it in the pocket of my sweats. Needless to say, it hasn't been seen since, despite a thorough search of every couch, bed, and pocket. That said, depending on the location of your piercings, there are some doctors that may allow you to sign a refusal form stating you understand the risks and they will just put tape over the piercings instead.

Decide who will be your driver. You must have

a ride home to be allowed to have the surgery; you will not be able to drive yourself. If you live alone, it would be good to have someone stay with you for the first couple of days and overnight until you get the hang of things.

If your surgery is long distance, you will also need to make all your travel, lodging, and transportation plans, and it becomes even more important to have a folder with all of your essential paperwork in it. Don't forget your ID/passport. If you anticipate walking through long airport concourses, arrange with the airline to have someone bring a wheelchair to pick you up. Even a week after surgery, one's body will tire quite easily.

Another consideration, if you are traveling for your surgery, is your luggage. Your arms, post-surgery, will have limited range of motion. Hopefully your luggage has wheels and your caregiver can assist you. Your carry-on should be lightweight, and it's a good idea to bring a travel blanket in case your temperature fluctuates. Take your pain medication and antibiotics on board with you—do not pack them in your luggage. This way, if your luggage gets lost you'll still be okay.

The other consideration I want to prepare you for is TSA. The body scanner, where they have people put their arms in the air? Um, you will definitely not be able to do that. This means you are going to have to talk to them and they will likely want to pat you down. TSA has been patting me down forever. You can ask for privacy and request a particular gender to do the pat-down. If you have the funds, it might be worth it to get TSA PreCheck, which may help you avoid the situation.

If you have a disability that requires the use of a manual wheelchair, you may want to find out about renting an electric one. You will not be able to maneuver a manual wheelchair right away. You may need more caregiver hours than usual, to assist with dressing and toileting, depending on your particular needs.

If you are going to apply for medical leave or disability, you may be able to do some of that paperwork up front. Pre-surgery is the time to look into that.

You will want to pack a gym bag or other small bag for your hospital visit, for three reasons. One is it will give you a place to put your clothes, wallet, and other stuff when they have you disrobe and put on a hospital gown. Two is that, while top surgery is usually an outpatient procedure, there is a chance that you will need to stay overnight in the hospital. Not to scare you, but there are many things that can happen during a surgery, and they might just want to watch you overnight, to ensure you are okay. Three is that you need something to put on after surgery. Pack a loose, soft button-down shirt, at least a size bigger than your usual, so it fits over the binder (I'll cover more about binders in the post-operative recovery chapter), or a zip-up hoody (it will be a while until you are able to lift your arms over your head to put on a T-shirt), and easy on/off pants—like your favorite sweats or pajama bottoms. When packing your clothes think about which ones make you feel safe and comfortable.

Other items include a toothbrush and toothpaste, underwear, slip on/off footwear/ slippers, your phone and charger, insurance cards, and copayment if needed. If you have someone with you, make sure they have a copy of your Advance Directive (even if they leave it in the car). I'll explain more about this very important document below.

For at least six to eight weeks after your surgery, you are not going to want to lift heavy items or move your arms above your head. And by heavy items, I mean anything more than five pounds. So, it's a good idea to prepare your home for this. Move all your everyday items to waist-level or lower— coffee mugs, plates, things in the refrigerator, your favorite hat in the closet, and so on. You may want to purchase a grabber for about $20, because you will not be able to raise your arms without cursing. Over stretching can also rip your stitches, creates additional bleeding and stretch your scars out. Remember while you're healing not to use only your dominant arm; use them both.

Collect some extra pillows, to prop yourself up in the bed or on the couch. Some people have even bought or rented a Lazy Boy chair for their recovery. My wife wanted to rent one, which at first I thought was ridiculous. We had a fight over this. Can you believe it? So, you'll have to decide for yourself on that one.

You should buy some things that help you with nausea, as pain medications might make your stomach a little queasy. For some people this might be ginger chews or ginger ale; for others, saltine crackers, bananas, or toast. The doctor may provide you with anti-nausea medications as well.

You won't be required to shave your pits for the surgery, but you might want to trim your underarm hair—if you have drains, getting the hair out of the way will be helpful. Notice I did not say to shave, just to trim. Most doctors do NOT want you to shave beforehand, because a razor causes little micro-traumas that can allow bacteria to enter the body, which increases the chance of infection. If you're on T and have some dense fur the surgical team might shave you, likely where they plan to make incisions.

It's also a good idea to put your support network in touch with one another before your surgery. Make sure they have one another's phone numbers and/or email addresses, so that if they want to check in with one another they won't have to rely to rely on you, as you might be resting, asleep, or gorked out on pain medication.

If you have small children, you need to consider arranging childcare, because you will be on pain medications, feel weak, will tire easily, and won't be able to lift them. The same goes for pet care.

Checklist—Home Tool Kit

- ✓ Grabber
- ✓ Bendable drinking straws
- ✓ Gauze pads
- ✓ Medical tape
- ✓ Wipes—organic, scent-free, flushable
- ✓ Antibiotic ointment
- ✓ Hydrocortisone ointment
- ✓ Handheld shower attachment
- ✓ Step stool if you have a high bed
- ✓ Downloaded movies
- ✓ Magazines, books
- ✓ Back scratcher
- ✓ Back sponge on a stick
- ✓ Laxatives such as Ducolax, Colace, and prunes
- ✓ Yogurt or probiotics
- ✓ Benadryl and Zyrtec to help with itching
- ✓ Throat lozenges
- ✓ Scar treatment of your preference
- ✓ Travel pillow for sleeping on your back
- ✓ Pill box
- ✓ Notebook and folder
- ✓ Plastic poncho for minimal showering
- ✓ Bed lap tray
- ✓ Ginger chews for nausea

You do not have to have these things, but they will make your life easier. And you don't have to buy all of this—you can pick up a few extra straws next time you eat out, you can ask the doctor's office for some extra gauze pads before you leave or at your follow-up appointment, you can ask friends to bring you magazines. Honestly, sleep is going to be your best friend those first couple of days.

My best advice: make yourself a big pot of homemade soup and freeze it before your surgery. Soup is not only warm and comforting, it has healing properties as well.

Advance Directives and Hospital Visitation Forms

You're going to want to skip this section. Don't. You are a responsible person. You want to do the right thing. This is the right thing.

Listen, I'm not trying to freak you out, but you should have these forms. Why? Because the world still discriminates. You are going to be involved with so many people along this journey, and it only takes one transphobic or homophobic conservative to make your life hell (can you say Kim Davis)?

An advance directive, living will, or health care power of attorney is a document in which you name someone who can make medical decisions for you, if you cannot make them for yourself. Say there is a complication—maybe you had a reaction to the anesthesia and were confused for a couple of days and had to stay in the hospital. Who would you want to speak for you? This document allows you to choose whom you want in this role and to write down what kind of treatments are acceptable or not. This is not about finances or assets; it only covers health care decisions. I promise that you will not be jinxed by filling this out—just the opposite, you will be protected and so will your loved ones. This is a simple free or low-cost way to protect your rights.

The regulations around advance directives, or living wills, vary state by state. Some HMOs can provide the form. Alternatively, do an Internet search for "advance directives" or "living wills" in your state. Nolo has a great website for reference (nolo.com), as does the Human Rights Campaign (hrc.org). Most state governments have designed these forms so you can fill in the blanks on your own and without an attorney. Some forms require one or two witnesses to sign. My preferred method is to go to one of those mailbox places and have it notarized.

The other form I want you to fill out is a hospital visitation form. My wife and I do not travel without it—in case of a medical situation in a discriminatory setting, we have this form to fall back on. If you have to stay in the hospital and some nurse in the middle of the night says "only family" can visit—even if you haven't spoken to your family of origin in years—and they won't let your wife in, you've got a document that says otherwise. It happens. Please be prepared. You can find a sample and create one for free at the Rocket Lawyer website (rocketlawyer.com). It's one page, and again, I like the idea of getting it notarized, but you can also use witnesses of your own, if they're around.

What I don't want you to do is get freaked out by all the talk on these forms about life-sustaining treatment and illnesses. You needing that level of care is about as likely as you winning the lottery, okay? The main thing I want you to have is an emergency contact person who knows you and cares about you and who can make decisions for you, if need be; and to have your visitation rights met, should you have to stay in a hospital. Give your chosen agent a copy, as well as the admitting nurse when you get to the hospital, and in the meantime keep a copy of the forms somewhere for safekeeping. This protects you during this surgery, but also after. You can change it anytime you want, so it's not a forever commitment. You'll feel all grown up.

If you've read this chapter and done what we've talked about, you're ready. You've got the tools you need and you're as prepared as you can be for the big day.

Chapter 6

Examining What Happens on the Day of Surgery

*M*y recommendation is to schedule your surgery first thing in the morning. That way you don't have to go as long without food and drink, and the surgeon and their team are fresh. On any given day, surgeons perform surgery after surgery after surgery. Do you want to be the last one of the day? No. You schedule your appointment in the morning, and then you let go.

Let me explain. Here you are, ready to go on your big day. You are so excited you're pacing, but you're also a little nervous—it is a big surgery, after all. The phone rings and the nurse on the other end says there's been a change of plans. This happened to me. "Sorry, the surgeon is running behind, we have to delay and reschedule you later this afternoon." What a letdown—but what can you do? Nothing. Breathe.

Just when I wrapped my head around that, the phone rang again. Can you get here NOW? Unfortunately, that's the way it is in the medical field. Things are unpredictable. Some people's surgeries have been rescheduled to the next day. That's probably the worst case, but it does happen, so be aware. I personally trust divine timing, figuring there is a reason for everything, and this helps me relax and go with the flow.

You can always take another shower while you're waiting. Whatever the case, enjoy your shower on the day of surgery, it'll be your last full one for a week or so. (Don't use deodorant, lotions, or powders.)

When we got to the hospital, I had to fill out more consent forms in the waiting room. Then my wife and I had two startles right off the bat. First, when the nurse came to get us she said, "This way, ladies." It is a mind fuck to go in to have male chest reconstruction and be referred to as a "lady." The nurse had my paperwork in hand so presumably she knew why I was there, but maybe not. I had also been told by my PCP that my chart was flagged as "transgender", okay maybe she didn't see that either. Isn't this the very system that labeled me with gender dysphoria? Well, being called "lady" does not help! I have heard of private plastic surgery offices where the waiting lounges were divided into male and female, and the person having top surgery was placed on the women's side without having been consulted. Awkward. And really there is just no excuse for not having a safe comfortable area for someone to wait.

The next startle was when another nurse came in to go over the procedure and said, "You're here for a double mastectomy and"—waving her hand over the paperwork—"all that other stuff." I surprised even myself by stating quite matter of factly, "Okay, I want to be absolutely clear that I am getting male chest reconstruction."

Do not let them get away with being vague. Speak up if you have to. You're going under, and you want to know beyond a doubt that everyone involved is on the same page. Though nice enough, this nurse was obviously uncomfortable to the point she couldn't verbalize my procedure. That is not okay. I have tried hard to teach diversity in hospitals, and occurrences like these are inexcusable. They can really shake a patient's confidence.

When you get into the room, you'll put your clothes in the gym bag you brought and put on that lovely hospital gown and warm booties, the kind with the non-skid Z patterns or paw prints on the bottoms. They will insert an IV into your arm, put on a blood pressure cuff, and put your hair in a net, which looks particularly handsome. But you won't care—your day is finally here, you have been through so much in your life, this is a piece of cake. If you are super anxious, they may even give you a little sumthin' sumthin' to relax you.

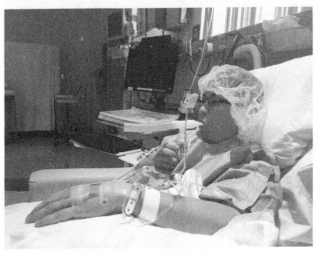

Preventative asthma treatment before surgery

Top surgery is usually an outpatient procedure. It can take anywhere from one-and-a-half to four-plus hours. You will be put under anesthesia, and it's unlikely that you'll need a catheter. Think of anesthesia as being asleep: you have bladder control while you sleep, and remember, you won't have had anything to eat or drink for at least twelve hours prior to your surgery. If, by chance, your surgeon wants you to have a catheter (you can challenge this and ask why), a tube will be put through your urethra into your bladder (while you are under anesthesia), then removed after you are awake and in recovery. It is not painful, but feels more like an annoying pressure.

You will have an IV put into your arm and blissfully go to sleep. Anxious? Afraid of needles? Tell the nurse and they will give you a little something to help you relax. When you wake up, you will have a new chest.

If there were any complications, they might want to keep you in the hospital overnight for observation. Not the end of the world, and better safe than sorry. You might want to find out in advance what your co-pay for an overnight will be, so you don't go into sticker shock on the spot. Most hospitals have payment plans, and some even have financial assistance, so be sure to request this, if the cost would be a financial burden.

The surgeon came in to see me before the procedure. It's a good idea to see your surgeon before taking any drugs in case you have any last minute questions. She lowered my gown and took out a purple marker. She drew dotted lines from my collarbone down. She drew incision lines above and under my breasts. Then she hung a tape measure around and over my neck and diagrammed where the new nipples would go and marked the old nipples to their new trimmer size. It didn't seem very scientific to me, more like freehand art. She stood back, took a look, seemed satisfied, and confidently said, "See you later."

Now here, my friend, is a photo op. My wife used the time between when the surgeon left and before the nurse returned to take a few pictures. I am so glad, because the before and after images still amaze me. If you have the opportunity I highly recommend taking two types of pictures now. Take one picture of you sitting up in the bed, holding the sheet in each hand and pulling it up to just cover your nipples. You'll still be able to tell a lot about what you looked like pre-surgery. Take another picture with the sheet down, fully exposing your soon to be history breasts (for yourself, if no one else). I actually use the picture with the nipples covered the most. That picture does not make me feel as vulnerable, but it definitely allows

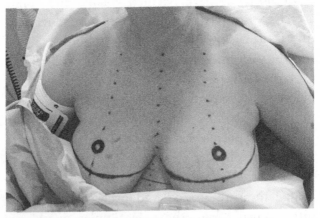

Surgeon's markings with new nipple placement

the viewer to see the dramatic change that took place. Since our society has a hang-up around nipples the partially covered picture is one I can show just about anybody.

I was surprised when a very close colleague

and friend told me a couple of months after I had shown her the pictures that she was "shocked" by the images (the no-nipple version). On a lighter note, another friend commented, "Oh, my god, I had no idea how big you were, you did a good job hiding those!" Well, yes, I did, thank you very much. The moral of the story: always, even with your closest friends, ask if they want to see the pictures first.

Before I left the hospital, the nurse in the recovery room asked if I wanted to peek at my new chest. YES, I did. She opened the bandages ever so slightly and I got my first look at the new me. I had an ear-to-ear grin; I was elated. I still remember the feeling. Then she bandaged me back up and gave me a frosty ice pack, which felt so good. She even generously gave me a couple of ice packs to use at home. Oddly, on my pre-surgery instruction sheet there was a mention of ice, but not on the post-operative discharge instructions. I used ice off and on only for a couple of days, until I found that anything touching my skin was an irritant. It was only at my follow-up appointment that the physician's assistant told me that one should never use ice on a nipple graft, because the cold constricts the blood flow to the new tissue! Yikes! So, unless otherwise told by your surgeon, do not use ice packs.

Before your ride home, it's a good idea to request an injection of pain medication and anti-nausea medication. Otherwise you are going to feel every bump in the road or you might get sick to your stomach or both.

So you made it through your surgery. Congratulations! You have a new chest! Now let's look at what happens afterwards.

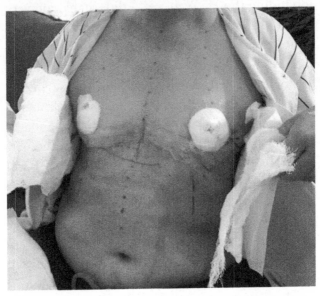

Adjusting binder for a quick peek on day of surgery

Chapter 7

Successfully Navigating Your Post-Operative Recovery

*B*efore you leave the hospital, you will be given discharge instructions, which will contain a list of the medications you are to take and what to do if you experience various symptoms, such as excess bleeding or fever. There will be phone numbers and follow-up appointment information as well. Keep track of these papers.

Forgive me for being redundant, but the first thing you are going to need to do is make sure you or your support person are writing down what medications you are taking, and when. Believe me, it all becomes a blur. It's just hard to remember when you had the last antibiotic, this pain med or that one, laxative, etc. Tip: The first couple of nights you should set your alarm and wake up and take your pain medication around the clock as prescribed. Every nurse I've ever known has told me that it's easier to stay on top of the pain than it is to play catch-up.

Pain medication is constipating, there's just no way around that. Use the laxative your doctor prescribes, but also know that if it's not working there are other laxatives available, so you should switch if you're not getting results. Don't go overboard by any means, but just be watchful. Two popular remedies for constipation are Colace and Dulcolax. The active ingredient in Colace is docusate sodium, which is a stool softener. It works by increasing the amount of water the stool absorbs in the gut, making the stool softer and easier to pass. Dulcolax's active ingredient is bisacodyl, which is a stimulant laxative. It works by increasing the movement of the intestines, helping the stool to come out. If one doesn't work, the other might. Both are available over the counter. It is also imperative that you stay hydrated to help avoid constipation, and of course natural remedies like dried fruits, especially prunes, are helpful. Munching on some popcorn, a cup of warm oatmeal, or a small bowl of rice, even a hot cup of coffee or tea might help you get things moving again.

As you may know, post-surgery you will likely be wearing a compression binder or compression vest (which is looser than a binder), or an ace bandage, depending on the type of surgery you had and your surgeon's recommendation. How long you need to wear this is variable; figure about three weeks. The binder holds your skin and tissue in place while your body heals, and provides some protection, which can be comforting. One complaint many have is that there can be areas on the binder that are rough and rub against your skin, causing irritation. If that happens, just put some gauze or a torn up T-shirt between your skin and the binder to provide a little extra padding.

You'll be sleeping on your back for a good six weeks, maybe longer. You won't be allowed to shower for about a week. The doctor will let you know about showering at the follow-up appointment. That doesn't stop some of us from using the handheld shower to wash the undercarriage or leaning over the tub so a caregiver can wash our hair. If you do, protect your new chest with a towel or rain poncho so no water gets on your chest. When you are finally allowed to shower, the spray will only be allowed to hit your back. You will not be allowed to soak in a hot tub or go swimming or even go into a pool for many months—wait for the okay from your doctor. The steri-strips that cover the incisions will start to slowly peel off; don't help them, just trim the loose tape ends off.

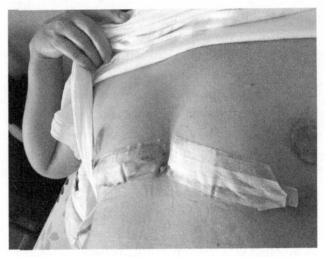

Steri-strips covering incisions will slowly peel off or surgeon will remove on follow-up visit

If you have drains, which is more likely than not, someone will need to help you with their maintenance. Drains are long thin tubes placed in your chest to collect excess blood and fluid, so it doesn't build up under the skin. They are connected to a small plastic bulb, one on each side of you, near your armpits. These containers will have to be emptied initially every 4-5 hours, less as days go by, and you can expect the container to start filled with fluid that looks rather bloody then lightens as the days go by. The surgeon may give you a log to keep track of the amount and frequency of fluid that is emptied. The drains usually stay in for three to seven days, and the fluid output is below 20-30cc. Since this is a sterile system, make sure you or the person helping you washes their hands before touching the drains or tubing. Drains can become occluded, or clogged, and if this seems to be happening, check your discharge instructions for how to unclog them or contact your physician.

You won't be able to drive while you are on pain medications and even for a while afterward due to your limited range of motion. Figure two weeks. Think about the seat belt (ouch) and how you turn the steering wheel—it's just too hard. On the way home from the hospital your caregiver can put the seatbelt on you because you will likely have some sort of binder to help protect you. My preference was to keep the shoulder strap away from my chest by hooking it to my thumbs.

You'll need to plan your life around not being able to drive, so make sure you have someone to run errands or take you to your follow-up appointment. Another option is to call a cab, Lyft or Uber. If you have a medical emergency such as uncontrolled bleeding, confusion or high fever of course you can always call 911. Don't wait that long though, call your doctor at any sign that things are not going as planned. Check your discharge instructions for more details.

No lifting over 5 pounds or reaching either. Overdoing it may result in a hematoma, which is when the blood vessel is damaged and blood leaks into the tissue. Reaching can stretch your incisions and cause bleeding or tearing of your new incision.

Did I mention no sex for three weeks? You don't want to risk causing any damage to the surgery site and honestly you probably won't have the energy as your body is sending everything it has to help your chest heal.

What you first see when the bandages are removed is not how your chest will ultimately look. Initially, I thought my incision lines looked very Frankenstein-like; my skin did not look like my own but looked almost plastic, like it was on some sort of living mannequin. I was shocked at the size of my round soccer ball belly and at the sight of two small moles under my right pectoral area that I swear I didn't know were there. My breasts had hidden parts of my body and distorted how I saw it. I didn't feel disappointed at all, just shocked by my mirror image, while simultaneously quite pleased.

But what if you are disappointed after surgery?

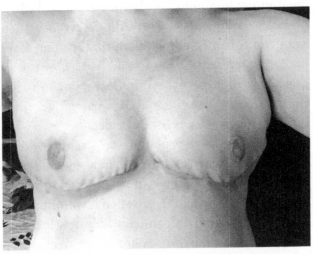

Frankenstein-like appearance diminished over time.

You see swelling and bruising and things don't look the way you had hoped? Each day, each week, your chest will heal and look better. However, there seem to be a few people, maybe you've seen their posts on the Internet, who are not happy with their outcomes. Perhaps they have big floppy dog ears by their armpits that don't go away with time, perhaps the nipple placement or scarring takes away from the aesthetic they were hoping for. Perhaps they lost one or both nipple grafts.

If this happens, you may be filled with anger toward the surgeon who botched your surgery; you may blame yourself for not doing better research or for overdoing it post-surgery. Your plan of action is first to let your body heal, and this takes time, six months at least. If after that time you are still not happy, you feel shame or embarrassment, then you must go for a revision. They can help. Yes, it will likely cost you more money, but you have not come this far to be unhappy with your body.

Emotionally, some people might feel more than disappointed but actually depressed after surgery. This could be related to the general anesthesia or pain medication. It could be due to the pain, discomfort and fatigue of the healing process and not being able to get back to your normal life right away. A lack of support after your surgery, for example having family or friends who are judgmental, can add to feelings of depression. If you have previously struggled with depression or anxiety it makes sense that you might have

81

these feelings post operatively. So, what to do? Remember that therapist who provided you with the letter saying you could get the surgery? If they feel safe, now is a great time to reach out to them. Call your surgeon's office and tell them how you are feeling. They have seen this before and may be able to offer some tips. Get out of the house and go for a walk. Get some sunshine. Call a friend and make a lunch date. Journal and get all those questions out of your head. Reach out. Look for a transgender support or social group. Check YouTube and other social media for stories similar to yours. Do not stay isolated and stuck. Being down and out is just temporary. You went through a big surgery and a big change. Reach out so others can help you get over the threshold and back in the game.

More on Post-Operative Healing

For several weeks after surgery, my chest felt something between a burning and a stinging sensation. The skin was extra-sensitive, and once the binder came off, I didn't even want a shirt touching it. The obvious solution was to go topless, which I happily did at home. Tylenol also helped. There was significant itching, which is common as the nerves reconnect, but it's crazy-making. It's not regular topical itching that you can scratch, it's itching deep inside that you can't reach. I asked my doctor about using hydrocortisone ointment and that was helpful.

As the healing continued, there were random stabbing pains. There were lots of numb spots on the incision site, which, over time, seem to be reducing. Gentle massage may help with blood flow, pain, and certainly helps with connecting us to our new bodies.

Scar treatment is not covered by insurance and is an expensive hidden cost. You cannot begin scar treatment until your incisions have closed. The degree of scaring you will have depends on the procedure you have, the skill of the surgeon, your genetics and being careful not to over reach for things and stretch your scars during the healing process. Treatment is usually from two to four months, though you won't know the final appearance of your scars for twelve to eighteen months.

Though there are people who swear by vitamin E, arnica, cocoa butter, bio oil, and aloe, clinical research supports using silicone as the most effective scar treatment. Silicone comes in gels and sheets which resemble long Band-Aids. I found that my skin was sensitive to the Maderma gel which has a perfumed scent to it and that the ScarAway gel never quite dried but remained tacky to the touch even hours after application. The sheets are washable and reusable for a time and can be cut to measure. I have read that some people have found 100 percent silicone lube for much cheaper than traditional silicone scar treatments, but I did not try this.

Underneath your scar it will feel like a rope or fat cord. Gentle massage, again only after the incision has healed, can help with smoothing this area out.

If you are on T, then you may be able to conceal your scars with chest hair. You can also get a tattoo, but you'll have to wait a year and clear it with your doctor. But what if we reframe the whole scar thing? Scars are a part of surgery. Is it possible that you might consider your scars a badge of courage, an act of stepping into who you are? What if these scars of ours connected us to an entire group of people? I invite you to try that on and see how it feels.

Your new incisions should not have direct sun exposure for quite some time (some surgeons recommend a year to avoid darkening of the scars). If you go topless, use the strongest sunscreen you can find.

Post-operatively, your body needs to replace fluid and repair tissues. As a certified nutritional chef, I believe in the power of food to help heal our bodies. I promise not to go into a long discourse here, but I do want to mention a few of the most important nutritional tools to have in your tool kit.

Protein

Protein contains amino acids, which aid in wound healing and keep your immune system strong.

It is found in eggs, cheese, yogurt, chicken, soy, almonds.

Vitamin C

Vitamin C makes a protein called collagen, which is needed for repairing tendons and ligaments, and healing surgical wounds. It also enhances white blood cell formation, increases antibody production, and helps metabolize anesthetics. It is found in citrus fruits, strawberries, kiwi, mangoes, watermelon, baked potatoes, broccoli, and bell peppers.

Zinc

Zinc may increase the speed of healing, and reduce inflammation, bacterial growth, and scar tissue creation. It's found mostly in animal foods (meat, fish, poultry, and dairy) also whole-grain bread and cereals, dried beans, and nuts. A high-dose supplement may cause nausea.

Vitamin A

Vitamin A is a potent antioxidant, enhances immune cell function, helps protect the wound against infection, and helps with healthy tissue formation. Found in cantaloupe, pink grapefruit, apricots, carrots, sweet potatoes, dark, leafy vegetables.

The Follow-Up

So, you're healing nicely and feeling better every day. You're getting up and walking around every few hours to keep the blood flowing. You're watching your body for any of those signs listed on your discharge paper—fever, red lines, hot spots, excessive bleeding, not being able to hold down food/water. You're taking your pain meds and antibiotics as prescribed and you slow down on the strong pain meds and switch to Tylenol (or whatever your doctor recommends) when you can. Looking good. Feeling good.

Your follow up visit will likely be 5-7 days post op. When I went back to the doctor's office for my follow-up visit, the person who took me into the room to wait for the doctor told me to remove my shirt and asked if I wanted a gown or not. I was caught off guard. I had never been asked that before. I said no and sat there proudly with my—albeit bandaged—chest exposed. You're going to experience some firsts.

I had bandages over my nipples, as you will if you have had a nipple graft. I was surprised to find that when the bandages were removed there was what looked like a foam compression pad actually stitched around my areola. This is called a bolster and it is used to hold the graft in place. The sutures were snipped and the pads removed, and there were my nipples—which also had sutures, though they were much harder to see. Those sutures stayed in, though, and sort of melted away, and I also pulled out a few strays as time went on. Your job will be to change the NAC dressing once a day and apply antibiotic ointment with a q-tip and a new gauze pad which will then be taped in place before you put on your binder. This will go on for about three weeks. You can expect some bleeding to continue and your nipples will eventually shed or peel in the third or forth week. That is normal.

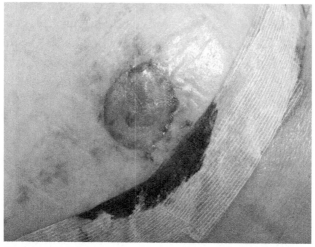

Healthy nipple graft

For many of us, the mirror has been something to avoid. It did not accurately reflect how we saw ourselves, and each time we saw our reflection, the mirror was a reminder of the dissonance we felt on the inside versus the outside. But now—oh, now, there has been a transformation. Even with bandages, even with pain and not able to use our arms completely, we can look and smile—finally, a body we can live in, feel, own. For some of us this will complete our journey; others will move on to take hormones if they don't already, and maybe have more surgeries to complete their vision of themselves. But here in the mirror, for many of us, is the first time we can look and we can see who we are and are becoming.

While I did feel high after surgery, I also felt very emotionally sensitive and vulnerable. Maybe some of that was due to the pain medications, but I suspect more of it was coming out on the other side of a huge portal. My heart chakra, if you believe in that kind of thing, felt like it had been opened in a new way. My heart was closer to the surface now, a little more exposed and accessible.

You may notice you are carrying yourself differently, shoulders back, head held higher. You are no longer curled forward, hiding your body. Confusion is replaced with a certain clarity and groundedness.

If you notice strain or tension or pain in a part of your body other than your chest, you might want to consider seeing a body worker or chiropractor. If you had large breasts, your body was accommodating them, and now will readjust after having them removed, so there is a sort of rebalancing. Definitely check with your doctor about when it is safe to have body work done. I went to my chiropractor four months after my surgery and felt it was beneficial. This can be expensive; however, you may be able to find someone who charges on a sliding scale.

Chapter 8

Removing the Binder and Making a Powerful Reentry

*B*efore I went back to work, my friends were texting me, asking if I wanted to be called by another name, and which pronoun to use. I thought this was very sweet of them. I hate pronouns. I've spent many years trying to avoid them, so I wasn't sure how to answer them.

When I went back to work, everyone who knew about the surgery was, naturally, staring at my chest. Those who didn't know assumed I had been on vacation and asked how it was. If I said, "Oh, I had some surgery," they would ask if I was okay. That was usually when I made the decision whether to disclose or not, based on how well I knew them, or the vibe I got from them (would they be respectful and supportive?). Sometimes I said, "Oh, it was elective. I'm fine, thanks for asking, so how are you?" and change the subject. Other times I actually explained what I had done, because just saying I had top surgery was met with a puzzled look. I remember one of the first doctors I told. He thoughtfully considered what I had said (no one ever expects you to say this, even if you did present as a masculine before your surgery) and then asked if I would be going on to take T or have other surgeries. Though quite personal, I actually thought that was pretty astute of him.

Prior to my surgery, I'd say I was assumed to be male, when I was out in the world, a little more than half of the time. Sometimes the person would give a subtle look down to my breasts, before I'd even said anything, and self-correct, "Sir—uh, ma'am." But I can tell you that when I started leaving the house after my top surgery, the number of people assuming I was male shot way up. I realized I had taken away a big physical cue.

I personally don't mind being referred to as male. If you're transitioning FTM, then you're going to be pleased by this. If you're non-binary and don't want to be referred to as "sir," you will have to come up with a strategy about how to handle this.

My first encounter with the world post-surgery was picking up my six-year-old daughter from summer camp. She introduced me to a little friend, who immediately turned to her and asked if I was her dad or her mom. Then, in a Target store, a little girl asked my wife if I was her husband, to which my wife said "Yes." The little girl responded neutrally, "Well, she talks like a girl!" Somewhere during those first few weeks of recovery, my daughter asked, "Do you have a wiener?" Clearly I had made things more confusing for people. I, however, felt AWESOME.

The bathroom situation got worse, though. I want to say I will always choose the men's room, but it's not that simple, as you know. I trust my Spidey senses regarding safety, and make up my mind in the moment. Post-surgery, I was at a restaurant and opted for the women's restroom. As I reached for the door handle, a male-appearing staff member literally lurched toward me and announced I was going into the wrong room. I don't blame him, really. We just need more gender-neutral bathrooms.

Chapter 9

Creating a Boundless Life

*P*owerful things can happen when your outside begins to align with your inside.

You have done something proactively positive. You are alive, perhaps happier and more in your body than you've ever been. You may see other changes that need to happen, to continue having things fall into alignment with the new you. You may finally feel in charge of your destiny.

You have gone through a portal. You see yourself and the world differently from this side of your surgery. Possibilities may open up that you could not see from the other side. You may spend time pondering your gender and what it means, which label, if any, you will take on or off, even which pronoun you want to use is up for grabs.

You will encounter many firsts, like coming out all over again. Who do you tell? Do you want to go topless at the pool for the first time? Will people stare, do you care? This may take some time to sort out. Afterall, you are just getting used to this new self reflection in the mirror. The new feelings in your chest, the ever changing look of your scars, the feel of someone's hand caressing your new chest for the first time, and the softness of your T-shirt. We are more than our surgery but our surgery has changed us.

First public exposure at a local hot spring

My friend Lee had this to say about his post–top surgery metamorphosis:

> I believe, for me, that choosing to go ahead and transition was the first time I had chosen to live

authentically and actually do something positive for myself. While that seems like it should be the catalyst for more change, I don't believe it actually started to manifest until top surgery, because the surgery itself is so visible. Yes, I had started testosterone about eight months before, and I was starting to see some changes, but as far as a dramatic change, the chest surgery was it. I was starting to try and understand exactly who I was in this new body. I had already ended my relationship with [my ex], partly because she was also struggling with her identity and was asking me not to identify the way I had chosen to (as a straight male). I no longer wished to appease people, as I had before—I wanted to really experience who and what I believed I finally was.

After surgery, the woman I was having a long-distance relationship with moved here and we began to live together. I can't really describe what it's like to finally have a lover be able to run her hand over my torso and not feel stressed out, angry, disgusted by myself. It was one of the most exhilarating experiences of my life. I no longer had to avoid touching myself or make sure that I moved a certain way to avoid contact. I was no longer half focused on avoiding my lover at the same time I was trying to get close to them. It was a whole new experience, much like having sex for the first time again.

I made a lot of choices from then on out. I quit smoking. I had smoked since I was in the fourth grade and I was now in my mid-thirties, and one day I was out smoking and this thought popped into my head: *Why are you trying to kill yourself?* I realized that most of the things I was doing with my life—smoking, overeating, not exercising, focusing mostly on work, not having fun—were all about how much I disliked myself and wanted to avoid life. So I started making those changes. I moved to a new state, because I wanted to try being in a whole new atmosphere. Eventually I was laid off and I went for a whole different kind of job, focusing on what I wanted to do, what I enjoyed, as opposed to what paid my bills or could buy this or that. We downsized a lot and had the absolute best time.

Exercising and food have been where I've struggled. I sort of go on binges, but I have gone from being a meat eater to a vegetarian to currently trying a raw vegan diet. I have lost weight and felt a lot healthier, from the diet changes and the walking I do daily, so that has made a difference in a lot of ways.

Mostly, though I have just strived to live a life that makes me happy, however that may look. I no longer try to fit in, or go with the flow, as it were. I really look at where I am and how I'm feeling about things. I want to be happy now, I want to enjoy life and I want to be who I am, whoever and however that may look. I no longer wish to conform, because I know when I tried that before it was slowly killing me, inside and out. Now I'm just me, and me is a pretty damn awesome place to be now.

Perhaps you have been holding onto a non-supportive partnership or friendship, perhaps you've been at a job you can't tolerate, perhaps you've been wanting to take on a creative project or learn something new. Well, your time is here. Do it. You are fearless. You are courageous. This is your time. Go ahead, define yourself. Choose love and hope and growth.

About the Author

Drake Cameron Sterling holds a Master's Degree in Social Work (MSW) with an emphasis on community mental health, and is a hospital social worker, author, and diversity educator. Drake's personal experience with top surgery, along with extensive experience as a healthcare patient advocate, led to the creation of *Top Surgery: Unbound.*

Want to get something off your chest? Join the conversation at TopSurgeryUnbound.com. You'll also find extras not included in the book.

Made in the USA
Monee, IL
02 February 2023

26797125R00069